Digital Fortitude: A Poetic Guide to CyberSecurity

Ashwini Siddhi

Presentation by *BookLeaf Publishing*

Web: www.bookleafpub.com

E-mail: info@bookleafpub.com

ISBN: 9789358739428

First edition 2023

DEDICATION

Dear Dad, I am forever grateful to you for instilling in me the courage to break through all glass ceilings. I owe everything to you.

A Tribute to My Mother, But a Warning for All

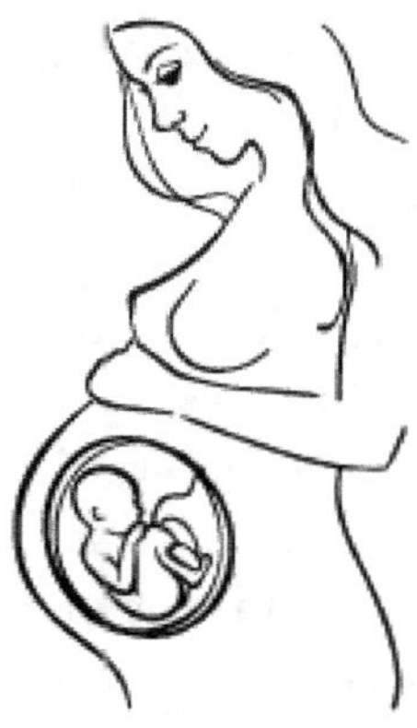

My mom, my heart's delight,
The most beautiful soul in my sight.
Her care and love, like a blooming flower,
Makes my heart beat with an eternal power.

I want the world to see her grace,
And post her pictures, in every place.
On her 60th, I wrote a rhyme,
Shared on Instagram, it felt sublime.
The comments poured in, sweet as candy,
It felt like I was a child so dandy.

But the bank's call left me in shock,
Someone tried to impersonate me, what a crock!

My mother's date of birth they knew,
And my personal information too.
It was hard to tell who could be behind,
My public profile, they could easily find.

I realized my mistake and made a change,
My privacy settings, I rearranged.
I unfriended strangers, deleted what's sensitive,
To protect my online presence, that's imperative.
It's tempting to share our world online,
But it comes with a cost, a risk so fine.
Remember, it's okay to keep things private,
And not over-share in the online riot.
For the things we most, cherish,
Are often in our hearts, sans blemish.

A Love Beyond Nudes

I met a boy, oh so pretty
And we've been going a while steady.
One day, he asked me for a photo nude
Made me blush and also brood.
After a thought and two
Told him with a sense of gloom..

Sending nudes seem like harmless fun
But once sent, can't be undone.
When the image is out of our hands
We can't control where it lands.
It could end up in the wrong person's sight
Or be used against us in a fight.
It's not worth the risk, it's plain to see
So let me keep my photos, where they should be.

He told me, I was right, and glad I had an
opinion so bright
 "You don't need nudes to be loved, or my angel,
to fly"
"I understand now, this aint being sly or oh so
shy"

"Your privacy is precious, let it not go waste"
"Let us not give in to peer pressure, and be in
haste"
"Your body is beautiful, and it's yours to
cherish,"
"Don't give it away, just to please and to relish."

I met a boy so pretty
And we've been going awhile steady.
Through ups and downs, we still have our fights
petty
But I met a boy so pretty, and we've been going
awhile steady.

Safe Travels

I love to travel to places far and wide
See mountains and seas, and get lost in the tide
Discover new cultures and find hidden spaces
Experience the unfamiliar, with open embraces

People always ask me, for tips to travel
But there's one rule that's crucial to unravel

When you land in a new place, and feel the urge to post
Connecting to public Wi-Fi, should not be your foremost boast
Rogue networks and man-in-the-middle attacks
Can leave you vulnerable with just a few hacks

Hacker stealing, may be lurking, or snooping on your content
A VPN's what you need, to stay secure and prudent.

So, travel with joy and be adventurous and free
But stay safe and secure, that's the key!

My Cyber Crush

I met a girl online, oh so pretty
She was dainty and feline, such a ditty
Talking to her was so much fun
My boring days, she made them undone

But sometimes she goes MIA
Leaving me wondering what to say
When she's back, everything's all right
Until she tells her story, of gloom and plight

I loved her and gave her my cash
Seeing her happy, I felt like a glowing flash
Days turned into weeks, but still no meet
Then I found out, I was the one being beat

She blocked me and vanished, never to be seen
Used someone else's identity, that's so mean
I was naive and my heart was broken
All my time and effort had been mistaken

Don't be like me, my friend, beware
Of fishy kitties with identities so rare

Don't give your money or your heart away
To someone online, who won't meet half-a-way
Protect yourself and be smarter than this
Or you'll end up just like me, in this abyss.

Sweet Sixteen's Bittersweet Surprise

On the day I turned sweet sixteen,
My father had to work, as was routine.
So I went out with my friends, to dine,
To a pop-up place, where we dressed so fine.

We savoured Italian food, oh so divine,
Ravioli and Tiramisu, oh what a find!
A sumptuous fare, beyond any true compare.

But the bill, it left me with a fright
My father's card, my means of might
I gave it to the waiter, with trust so high,
But his long absence left me with a sigh.

Days passed and now my father's account was
low,
The bank informed us of a card-skimming blow.
The waiter had taken the card and code,
Left us with a burden, heavy to uphold.

But our loss was saved by the card's limits set,
We'll never forget the thief's actions, yet.
So learn from me, and keep your card in sight
Or else you'll be a victim, of this terrible plight.

The Phishing Well

In the midst of the night, when slumber evaded
sight
I received an email of eerie might.
Full of grandiose promises, and cringe-worthy
claims
Urged me urgently to reveal my bank account,
and names.

Too excited to think, I clicked on this embedded link
Unaware, my safety was on the brink.
I entered my information with no clue
Of the nefarious plans that would ensue.

My bank account now lies drained
Alas, my reputation strained.
I wish I had just hit "delete", and moved along
Instead, here I am worried, all night long.
This scam now, plagues my every thought
A mistake made, lessons learned, battles fought.

Remember, phishing is just a scam
It can be on SMS, email, WhatsApp, damn!
Don't be fooled, don't take that bait
Or you will be sorry, it's not too late!

Pup's Password and Sister's Steals

My sister swirled in dresses so fine
Showing off her online steals, divine.
Her words of thanks, I thought were sweet
But little did I know of her sneaky deceit.

She used my account to buy her spoils,
Deceitful ways hidden under her smiles.
When I inquired how she did it so,
She disclosed my password, oh no!

She knows my love for our dog so true,
A little bundle of joy, small and brown too.
He awaits me every day, with his tongue out,
And licks my face all over, with a happy shout.

My buddy, my friend, my furry delight,
I can't imagine being without him at sight.
In his honor, I use his name in passwords true,
But my sister smartly tried all combinations, to
break through.

My sister's dresses I don't mind,
But it could be someone else, we can't find.
So be smart and don't name your password with
ease,
On your love, be it a dog or a girl, stay safe,
please.

Juice Jacking: A Hacker's Stealthy Pursuit

I am a hacker and I revel in fun
And yes, I also hack for money, some
I vend your data on the dark web, my share of
gold
My skills are sharp, my deeds are bold

If someone asked, what is my favorite hack?
I'll tell you, I work at the local car rental shack
They earn big bucks, but give me small
Yet, I'm not worried, I have a trick that's tall

Each time a car is rented and the driver connects,
Their phone to the USB port, without regrets
I download their data and extract the juice
They remain unaware, mere sitting goose

This juice jacking is my succulent secret
I hope the users never learn to protect
To delete their data with care
Or to stop syncing their phones, a despair
I hope the users never know
To use their chargers, else the data they can forgo
They ought to provide minimal privileges to app
And avoid the risk of hacking traps
But until then, I'll keep on with my ways
Of hacking for fun and hacking that pays.

Promises to My Sister: A Vow of Protection

My sister, she's a shining star,
So smart and hardworking, by far
With a new job, she's on the rise
And with her first pay, a grand surprise

A laptop, brand new and sleek
She gifted me, my spirit did peak
But before handing it over to me
She laid down terms, three as can be

To use Anti-Virus, and update it well,
No random apps, no pirated sell,
Only from official providers, I shall trust,
And keep all software up-to-date, as I must.

My sister, my mentor, my guide,
an ethical hacker with a virtuous fire,
I strive to follow her path, and abide,
by her principles, which I deeply admire.

Share with Care

Sharing is caring, a phrase so true,
When happiness and grief we share with you.
Knowledge and food, we share with delight,
But some things are better kept out of sight.

Toothbrushes, unmentionables, and more,
Should be for one, and one alone, we implore.
Hygiene is key, it keeps us safe and sound,
And cyber hygiene is just as profound.

Passwords, OTPs, links, all secure,
Keep them to yourself, that's for sure.
Sharing them puts you at great risk,
Compromising your cyber immunity, it's brisk.

Phones and laptops, lock them away,
Don't let them be easy prey.
Survival of the fittest, Darwin said it best,
Be strong, be smart, adapt to the rest.

In the pandemic, hygiene was a must,
Cyber hygiene is no different, it's just.
Don't wait for an attack, to learn and be aware,
Take steps now, to safeguard what's yours with
care.

Secure Shopping: Navigating Fashion's Grand Reach

Fashion is art and I'm the canvas to wear,
A statement made with each thread and pair,
A creative outlet, a designer's flair,
An expression of self, beyond compare.

With just a click, the world's at hand,
Fashion's reach now truly grand,
No distance too far, no store too small,
Online shopping has made it all.

Online shopping, it beckons with ease,
Yet hidden dangers, a shopper's unease,
Pitfalls aplenty, money lost with a breeze,
But with tips, shopping can still bring us peace.

Brand's verified social media, handle is the key,
Visit the links they share, it's plain to see,
Don't browse search engines, for that's risky,
Use a separate card, with a limit low & picky.

Don't save card details, or you'll regret,
Breached websites, a danger you can't forget,
Deals too good to be true, better to ignore
Stay Safe, Happy shopping and more.

Identity and the Power of Paper

Sensitive documents, hold them tight,
PAN, Aadhar, Voters ID, with all your might,
Sensitive documents, they tie to your name,
ID cards, they hold your financial claim,
Random sharing, do not play that game,
Identity theft, it could bring you shame.

Don't give them out, just anywhere,
Online shopping, or random pub affair,
Ask for the reason, specific and clear,
Share only if justified, don't give into fear.
When asked randomly for IDs, do not comply,
Without good reason, don't let them pry.

Your right to reject, it's the law,
Protect your identity, leave no flaw,
Do not be a victim, you're worth more,
Keep your data safe, let your guard roar.

Identity theft, a haunting thought,
A nightmare scenario, so highly fraught,
Keep your documents safe, keep them near,
It's your security, do not veer.

A Bard's Password Sonnet

Oh, passwords! Safeguard of my digital life
In this age of hackers and constant strife
Crafted with care, thy strength is my shield
Against those who seek to breach and wield

Change thee, my dear password, at a steady pace
For constant renewal shall keep thee safe in
place
Thou art unique, not to be shared or told
Else, thy security may falter and unfold

A different password for each account I create
So that if one be breached, the rest stay safe
Oh, how sweet the thought of security assured
From the perils of the internet, we're insured

Thou art my ally, my guardian, my friend
With thy help, my online presence shall never
end
And so, I shall craft thee strong and hard to
guess
For in thee lies my digital life's success.

Passed the Quiz, Failed the Test

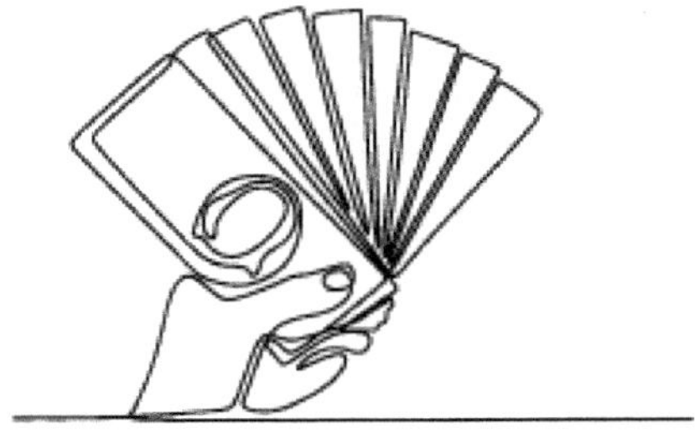

Sitting in an online class, oh what a bore
My friend's absence leaving me with wanting
more.

As the lecture is on, my mind takes flight
And wanders to the internet's vast sight
I stumble upon quizzes, oh so fun and bright
To find which breed of dog I would be, what a
delight!

My details I enter, for amusement and jest
Results so funny, I share with the rest
Hooked on these quizzes, I crave for more
To my personal information, I paid little heed
before

A wise friend alerts me to the malice and guise
Of quiz companies and their dark disguise.
My information sold for marketing or worse
In my naivete, I failed to perceive the curse

But now I know and will teach others too
To guard their details and avoid this rue.
So let us all be wary, and keep this in mind
Do not heed such quizzes, a task assigned
Never enter personal details, with no valid
reason
And keep our digital life safe, through every
season.

Steps and Stalks – A tale of geo-locations

I believe I have the gift of life's everything
A hack that many are yet to bring
I hit the gym every morning, later savor leisurely coffee's taste
And evening runs in the park, I make haste

I feel compelled to share these joys on social media's stage
To inspire others to turn a new page
But I failed to see the peril in my feed
Geolocation tags of the gym, home, and coffee's breed

The gym, coffee shop, and home, all on display
A stalker followed my every move, day by day
I had to quit the things I loved, my folks were mad
Mental trauma that followed, oh, it was bad

I reported to cops, they took some action
But the mental trauma was difficult to ration
This is a hard lesson, I learned with dismay
Not to share your location, in the moment or at
play

Not only for everyday life, but for travel and fun
Wait to post photos until you're on the run
Let the geotags be generic in name
This is a hide-and-seek game, don't play it for
fame
Better be a step ahead, if you want to win
In this digital world, guard your privacy like kin.

My Phone, My Rules

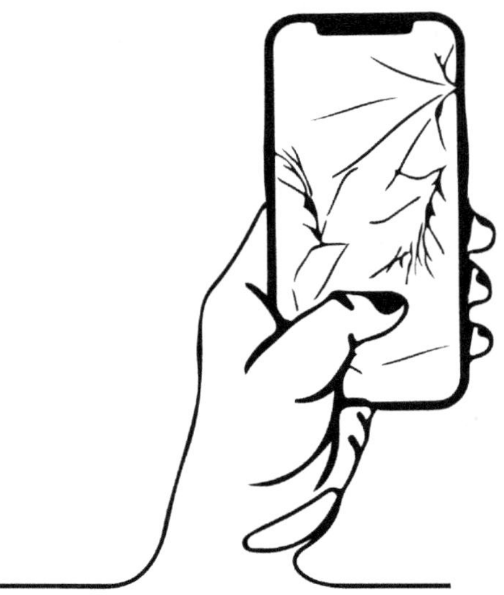

Today I strolled into the Banana Store new
And purchased a phone, shiny and blue
With hard-earned money, I value it true
And intend to use it in the best way, through and
through

I'll ensure no apps snoop on my privacy
App-access to microphone, camera, location, all
will be a rarity
Apps with least privileges, I'll give no charity
For I am the owner, with power and authority

No downloading of content, without my consent
No random additions to social media groups, I
resent
Before sharing my location, the app must
represent
And ask for my permission, with clear intent

Unnecessary numbers, I'll never save
Passwords for new apps, I'll always have
Authorize every payment, that's the deal
And leave no opportunity for apps to steal

Wi-Fi, Bluetooth, and Airdrop, off they'll be
Used only when the need arises, it's the key
Data protection settings and antivirus, a
guarantee
To keep my phone safe, as safe can be

I'll use VPN, never jailbreak
My phone's security, I'll never forsake
And lastly, the latest patches I'll take
To keep my phone updated, for security's sake

So here's my ode to my Phone true
And how I'll keep it safe, like any wise
tech-savvy crew.

My Poor Conning Friend, Melting in the Heat

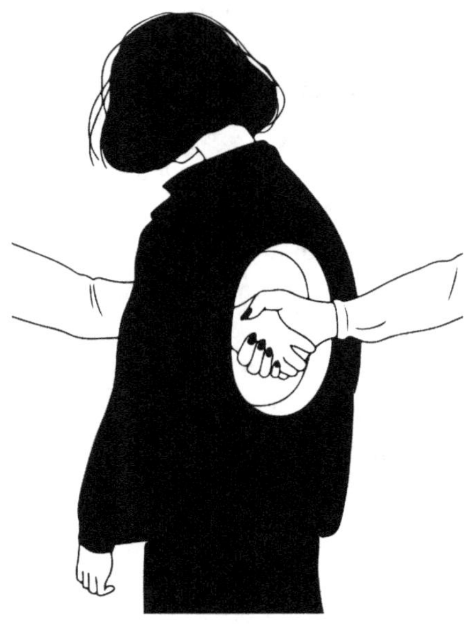

I sought relief, on this day of sweltering heat
With a friend, I went out to fetch a treat
An ice-cream in hand, we savored its delight
Chatting about our day and random things in
sight

Suddenly a message pops up on my app
Saying she's stuck and needed cash, asap
I looked at her confused, for she was by my side
What is this? My mind taking me on a ride?

In no time, another call came in to check on her
state
We knew something was off, it was a hacker's
bait
Her account was hacked and he was after some
dough
Lucky she was by my side, or else who knows

We reported the app and the customer service
team
They are now investigating this fraudulent
scheme
This incident made me realize, never trust an
online friend
If they ask for money, be sure to check till the
end

Always call them to confirm or reach out to
someone they are close
Don't fall for the hacker's trap, don't let them
impose
Let this be a lesson for all to learn
To double-check with the friend on a different
medium, stern.

My Friend, My Teacher and My Inspiration

Living in a hostel, surrounded by hills,
I miss my home, yet my heart fills
With new friends and memories to make,
Sharing rooms, clothes, and tech to take.

Yesterday, our projects were due,
We all submitted on time, our hard work true.
But today, my teacher called my name,
Said my project was identical, what a shame!

I claimed it was mine, but so did my mate,
The teacher was torn, had to decide our fate.
She gave us both a zero, oh what a blow,
I cried all day, watching my hard work go.

Then came my cybersecurity teacher,
She analyzed the work, said I was the keeper.
The other boy was punished, and my marks were
restored,
My heart filled with happiness, my spirits
soared.

She also gave advice, which was smart,
To never leave behind any work or docs, that's
just a start.
Store it in a password-protected drive, she said,
To keep it safe on shared devices, away from
prying heads.

Sensitive transactions on shared devices are a
no-go,
And always log out, before passing it to and fro.
My cyber security teacher is amazing and smart,
I aspire to be like her, with a kind heart.

Back-Up Photographer with Attachment Issues

My passion lies in photography,
Traveling places, capturing memories in
imagery.
With AI, I create beautiful scenes,
Like a fairy tale, a world of dreams.

An email came in from an unknown,
Saying they liked my photo and wanted to use it
as shown.
With haste, I had to consent,
And downloaded the attachment they had sent.

Excitement filled me, my dream coming true,
But then my screen went blank, and my heart
felt blue.
A malware was embedded in the attachment
they had sent,
And I realized my mistake, far too late to
prevent.
I had acted too fast, no verification made,
My device now compromised, and my files at
risk, laid.

Thankfully, my backup saved my day,
And my important data was not thrown away.

From this experience, I learned two things anew,
Never download exes no matter who or
attachments without verifying who,
And always backup your data, so you don't lose,
you.

Linked in Digital Chains

In today's world, social media reigns
Our identity entwined with these digital chains
To protect your data, a trick you should know,
Easy to follow and simple to show.

Check Whatsapp, Facebook, and every app,
The devices linked setting, a crucial map.
Take the lead, don't hesitate or wait,
See how many active devices on this date.

If any device seems strange or fishy,
Click 'Log Off' on it, easy-peasy
The app on your current device will as is run
Enjoy your browsing, it's fun.

Cookies, Consent and Control

As you browse on a random site, take heed,
When cookie consent pops up, don't concede,

Take a moment to review, only allow what's
needed,
Don't simply accept all, unheeded.

It may take a second or two more,
But it'll save you hours of headaches galore,

Cookie consent is your right,
Not a random hindrance, in your digital flight.

So review and allow with caution and care,
And safeguard your online data without despair.

Epilogue

Security is a duty, privacy a right,
Two sides of the same digital fight.
In the online world, we must be vigilant and bold,
To protect our data, both young and old.
Hackers and scammers abound,
Our sensitive information to confound.
But with awareness and knowledge, we can collectively prevail.
And keep both our privacy and security in full sail.
Remember, Security is a duty, privacy a right.

www.ingramcontent.com/pod-product-compliance
Lightning Source LLC
LaVergne TN
LVHW010829200726

843508LV00012B/2539